BURNOUT

Deal With It

KEITH MATTHEWS

First edition 2024

I would like to dedicate this book to all healthcare workers, teachers, and first responders who work hard serving the public every day with little regard for themselves.

I would also like to dedicate this book to Dr Julie Graves, who gave me the help, strength and support to bring this book to you.

Acknowledgements

I would like to acknowledge the women and men who came before me, mentored me, and taught me how to be a better nurse, father, and man. I would also like to acknowledge the patients and parents of patients who put such a sacred trust in my hands. I feel truly honored and blessed by the faith you have shown and taught me.

Table of Contents

Introduction

Burnout is pervasive across many professions in modern-day society. It triggers immense stress, costs businesses countless millions each year, and brings forth a range of health and psychological challenges. Its impact stretches into personal and professional realms, often eroding the joy of living a truly satisfying life. If you've ever faced burnout, you understand these truths all too well.

This book addresses 'burnout' from a healthcare professional's perspective. While no book can be a complete cure guide for burnout, the system presented here can help anyone control what they can control. This approach can make a difference for many professions when applied. I sincerely hope it helps you.

In this book, I reference aspects of healthcare work that aren't covered in school. I hold no ill will toward educational institutions; most do an admirable job fulfilling their primary mission of producing competent graduates who can pass licensing exams and enter their fields with the necessary technical skills and knowledge. However, schools often fall short in preparing students for the potential—and some would argue inevitable—burnout that can arise in these professions; there is little incentive for them to address this gap. Schools create a competitive entry environment to search for the best candidates, meaning those who have demonstrated a better-than-average or superior ability to learn. Schools are rated based on the number of entry-level students who successfully graduate from the program and pass the board exams, preferably in the first go.

These competitive institutions aren't evaluated based on their graduates' long-term success or career longevity. Addressing the full spectrum of challenges students will face—including the potential for burnout—might deter some from entering or completing the program. This would counteract their primary objective: to graduate a high number of soon-to-be licensed professionals. It's not that professors and institutions lack concern, but simply put, there is little financial incentive to address these issues. The end result is that many students are graduating with the basic knowledge and skills to do the job, but as I will demonstrate, not all have the survival skills needed to have long, successful careers.

This book is meant to help address that gap and help those who find themselves lost in the field, already burned out.

Having spent nearly forty years in the healthcare field. When I started, I thought burnout was what happened to less resilient people. I was strong, I thought, so it could not happen to me. Now, I can say without shame that I have experienced burnout regardless of how strong I was, thought I was, or am. Many times, I have gone through periods of excessive drinking, self-neglect by simply ignoring my health, comfort eating, and obesity; I have navigated life through two divorces. I have been, at times, an emotionally absent father. I have gone through periods of not wanting to be around people who "wouldn't understand." It is that silent understanding between healthcare workers, police officers, and first responders. You don't even have to ask; you can recognize someone in these professions; it's the silent understanding when you are a part of the group. Though not all my actions and reactions can be attributed to burnout, looking back, I can see burnout was the major factor.

I have survived and can report now thriving without even the hint of burnout. I now look forward to my day and my next shift adventure. I love people again. I have recaptured the joy that brought me to this field many years ago.

In this book, I will show you how you can avoid and defeat burnout.

I: Hero Tom

"Burn bright, not out."

— Hamza Khan

Tom (not his real name) was one of those nurses who drew everyone's attention – a truly magnetic person who seemed to touch everyone. Regardless of the unit or location in the hospital, you either knew Tom or knew of him. If you knew Tom, you respected and admired him, and as a young, wide-eyed newbie like I was then, I wanted to be like Tom.

He was a former Vietnam veteran who had served as an army medic. I was never certain whether he had been deployed "in the country" or not. As is typical with soldiers who have been in such situations, Tom never really discussed that period in his life. This was especially common with the veterans of the highly divisive war in Vietnam. While I wouldn't say he was a superhero in my young, impressionable mind, he was undoubtedly one of my early mentors and an endless source of knowledge about nursing and life.

Tom guided and inspired me to discover my inner passion for healthcare and showed me that it was okay to be a man in what was a female-dominated profession. He demonstrated that it was okay to be caring, empathetic, and compassionate, which were not widely accepted concepts for men at the time - the 1980s. He had a commanding yet kind presence when you spoke to him. In every conversation, I seemed to learn something about nursing or life. It felt as though I knew his wife and three children, whom he would often brag about and would manage to weave into every conversation. I left those interactions feeling better about myself and humanity in general. A man is a man, non-judgmental on every level; he seemed to always be in control. Nothing fazed Tom. To know him was to know a kind, compassionate, tough-as-a-nail, all-around good guy.

Even today, when I am in certain situations or faced with specific patient care scenarios, I still use some of his tips and out-of-the-box techniques. Even after all these years, I still sometimes hear his distinct, reassuring voice in my ear. I'm sure you have worked with or will encounter a nurse like Tom—someone who exudes confidence and is ready to share his or her knowledge. Someone who instills confidence, someone who naturally draws others towards them.

Tom's primary role was in the trauma intensive care unit, but whenever things were slow in his unit, he would come to help or hang out in the emergency room while many other nurses would disappear for a cigarette or television break. (Yes, those were the days when it was not uncommon for healthcare workers to smoke cigarettes, even at the nurses' station. I would have to look twice at the coffee cup I picked up to be sure it was mine and not someone else's ashtray. Let's just say mistakes were made.) So, while most would find a place to relax or hide, Tom would come to the ER, where the action was, to assist in any way he could. If no one needed help, Tom would engage in conversations with the staff, first responders, and police officers- anyone who had the time to spare. Tom was never a distraction, never an unwelcome guest. His presence just made everyone feel better.

Observing Tom in action when trauma patients arrived in the emergency room was like watching a conductor or a lead player in an orchestra—a vital component of an incredibly well-oiled machine. He always knew exactly what to do and when to do it. He would lend a helping hand to newcomers or anyone who seemed lost, guiding them back on track without harshness. Again, nothing seemed to faze Tom or get him out of focus.

Our hospital was the regional trauma center located in one of those older, post-industrial regions in the north. The area consisted of blocks of early-century row houses with brick facades—narrow and tall, constructed with tinderbox wood and old horsehair insulation secured by thin wooden lathing, covered with old plaster, with cinder block walls dividing the houses. These were, sadly, natural chimneys in design. These buildings had outdated wiring and copper plumbing, and the majority of blue-collar residents could never afford modernization. Although charming in appearance, this setup was a recipe for disaster. Every winter, our brave and selfless police and first responders would be called to one or more of these houses due to fires that seemed almost inevitable. It amazed me then that such incidents didn't occur with more frequency.

Unfortunately, one such incident happened on a cold, snowy night. A family was using a kerosene heater, which was common in those days. Kerosene was a cheaper alternative as a heating source for those families that could not afford to replace or resupply the old standard furnaces that ran on expensive heating oil. As was all too common, a family member had left a jacket by the kerosene heater to dry so that they had a warm, dry jacket in the morning to face the cold. As the family slept, the jacket ignited, and a fire broke out. The call went out that our hospital would be receiving a family of victims, brought in by the brave first responders who fought their way through the smoke and flames to bring out anyone they could find. It was an all too familiar high-volume, mass casualty event. One of these scenes would appear chaotic and disorganized to an outside observer, but in reality, it was a well-coordinated, highly trained team working with incredible efficiency to help people as quickly and efficiently as possible. It was like an orchestra in unity, somehow playing improv jazz.

Treating fresh burn victims, especially when there are more than one, is one of the more emotionally challenging scenarios in the healthcare setting. These individuals experience excruciating pain that is difficult to catch up to, let alone alleviate. Amidst the brutal sights, agonizing groans, and the smell of burnt clothing mixed with burnt hair and flesh, these experiences are some of the more challenging that can haunt you and are seemingly unforgettable. On this particular night, while preparing for the incoming patients, I remember Tom, as usual, taking the lead. Ensuring everyone was in their proper places, the expected equipment was present and in working order, and the bandages, medications, and so on were all present and ready to use. All relevant team members notified Tom was in his element.

Tom's familiar booming voice was absent as the scene unfolded with its inevitable mix of sights, sounds, smells, and adrenalin. Focused on the task at hand, it seemed no one noticed at first. However, some team members did notice and eventually had a moment or two to look for Tom. They found him curled up in a fetal position, holding his knees to his chest, rocking back and forth on the floor in a corner. A few colleagues went to help him. I remember he was at first inconsolable, flinching at every loud sound as if shocked by a jolt of unwanted electricity. Eventually, in the typical healthcare worker's fashion, they were able to help and console Tom.

Not long after this event, I moved to a warmer climate and never saw Tom again. I still don't know what became of him or whether he was able to continue his nursing career. Nevertheless, I will always remember Tom as a strong, compassionate nurse with a booming, loving voice who was always willing to assist others with anything within his power. A man who seemed to live life fearlessly, projecting extreme masculine pride, who would never allow himself to show any signs of weakness or vulnerability.

Here's to Tom, a true hero.

II: Who Wants to be the Hero?

"Only a life lived in the service of others is worth living."

— Albert Einstein

There's no single answer, as each person is driven by their unique motivations. However, certain traits are common among healthcare workers and first responders: a profound sense of empathy, deep compassion, and a selfless commitment to helping others. We thrive on the challenge of pushing ourselves while working within a team, united by a goal greater than personal gain—a goal focused on the well-being of others. Though we might be too humble to admit it, we deserve to see ourselves as heroes, not just individuals but as part of a collective of humble heroes.

While some may mistakenly believe that becoming a healthcare worker or first responder will lead to riches and fame, the reality, obviously, is quite different. These fields have advantages beyond helping people, such as a sense of job security and mobility. Open any job search engine for almost anywhere in the modern world, and you will see endless opportunities - you can go just about anywhere you desire and find a job as a healthcare worker, all while feeding the adrenaline and service junkie within you. The healthcare field provides some level of stability even during economic downturns, adding to the appeal of the profession. However, as a general rule, what truly drives healthcare workers and first responders is a burning desire within their souls—the desire to make a difference, be a part of a team, and help people. To save the world, so to speak. There are many other service industry professionals, experienced salespeople, internet entrepreneurs, and so on that offer the other intangibles, but there are very few other civilian professions where the priority is based on helping others in such a vulnerable, life-and-death time of need. Regardless of a person's wealth, social status, cultural or economic background, when working in an emergency room, ICU, or responding to a 911 call, the need of the person takes precedence. Healthcare workers and first responders have the unique blend of skill, opportunity, and desire to help any and all people during their most vulnerable moments. Few other professions profoundly impact people's lives, for veritable strangers and the lives of their families and loved ones.

Being a healthcare worker or first responder challenges each individual. It forces them to continually learn, grow, and keep up with the latest medications and procedures to save and enhance lives while expanding themselves. The joy and satisfaction derived from working in the healthcare field are unparalleled. It's an emotional and spiritual high that would be next to impossible to find elsewhere. Despite the pitfalls you will encounter, which I would argue, if properly prepared, you can avoid, I would strongly encourage those of you called to do so to pursue them with vigor and commitment. These really are great and rewarding professions, and your desire to be a first responder or healthcare worker is honorable.

As a general rule, people who seek these professions strive to help ease suffering, alleviate pain, and share the knowledge gained, ultimately with the goal of making a difference. However, entering these fields can be challenging. For instance, nursing requires meeting numerous college-level prerequisites just to apply for nursing school, and you better have excellent grades. Competition for limited spots can be fierce.

Becoming a hero demands discipline, sacrifice of social activities, time spent away from family and friends, and accumulating quite a bit of student debt with most people. Once admitted to nursing school, there are at least two more years of intense schooling and clinical practice, putting the rest of your life on hold. By 2022, the average nursing school graduate had over $23,000 in student debt and dedicated a minimum of four years to embark on this honorable and selfless journey. The numbers are very similar for any first responder. These are difficult, challenging journeys.

As with teachers and a few other professions, we dedicate ourselves to helping others at the expense of potentially pursuing more lucrative careers using our skills and talents. We do it because we care; we do it to shine. We do it to serve. It's not hard to imagine what lies in the hearts and minds of those who choose these professions, whether as police officers, first responders, or healthcare professionals.

Nursing schools. From their collective perspective, these schools aim to produce functional nurses who can competently care for people in the workplace. These schools are graded by the number of graduates they can produce as compared to the number enrolled, as well as by the percentage of those graduates who pass their nursing board exams, preferably on the first try. Their job is to focus on keeping students motivated and to graduate. Low graduation rates tend to reflect poorly on the school, making it more difficult to remain financially viable. Consequently, admission standards are high, and acceptance is fiercely competitive. Schools tend to select those who have demonstrated discipline and academic potential in the past. Emotional screening does not factor into this. The licensing boards measure your knowledge, not whether you are prepared for what you will see and experience. I won't say the people who run the schools do not care; however, there is little time and no incentive to address this in the screening process or curriculum.

To explain this another way, nursing schools teach the technicalities of nursing and medicine, instilling a sense that with the tools provided, one can save the world or at least positively impact the lives of those they encounter, feeding the common desire of those drawn to the profession. However, they do not prepare students for what to expect as a nurse—the negative outcomes, the stressors they will inevitably face, or how to cope with these factors. This is a major flaw in the system. If there are schools that address this, kudos to you; however, I am not aware of any.

After graduation, when nurses enter their first job, statistics indicate that even before the COVID-19 pandemic, approximately 17% quit or left the profession within the first year and 56% within the first two years, all while carrying a mountain of student debt. It costs a lot to hire and train a new nurse, so part of the ripple effects of this are less experienced staff, staffing issues, and ultimately huge costs to the system, which are then passed on to consumers. It becomes evident that these nurses and providers were never fully prepared for what they would encounter and experience.

These numbers also hold similarly true for first responders and police officers, although precise national statistics for police officers are challenging to obtain since most data remains regionalized. The best estimate suggests that around 50% of police officers leave the profession within the first five years, and for first responders, 50% in three years, according to the Bureau of Labor Statistics. Suffice it to say, these professions, chosen for their ability to change and touch lives, are often abandoned way too soon.

As I have shown, being a healthcare worker or first responder offers numerous personal and professional rewards that would be difficult, if not impossible, to replicate elsewhere outside of military service. All three provide the opportunity to work both individually and as part of a well-oiled, disciplined team, fulfilling the desire for camaraderie, teamwork, cohesion, and connection that we all crave to some extent. There is job growth and a sense of security, and although it may not make one rich, it ensures you won't be hungry. It may sound cliché, but when things are going right in any of these fields, we can hold onto the joy and soul satisfaction that led us into this profession. We simply love it.

So, what causes so many to give up on these professions so quickly shortly after entering the field? As I've observed and experienced, the answer is what is commonly called 'burnout.'

While some individuals may have other reasons, burnout is by far the most common cause. In the following chapters, I will delve further into this topic. I will argue and demonstrate that by focusing on the pure joy of being a healthcare worker or first responder—helping others in their greatest time of need, working with a team of selfless professionals—and learning to release and not repress the inevitable undesirable outcomes, we can overcome and not hold onto the pain, suffering, and possible demise of those which we could not relieve.

These experiences, if not dealt with and confronted, will linger in our subconscious, pricking at our souls like needles. It's akin to death by a thousand cuts, as I've experienced personally and heard from others in similar situations. We must remove the needles, become impenetrable to them, and hold on to the joy. Yes, my hero friends, you can do this.

Let's explore burnout in more depth.

III: Suck it up, Buttercup

"They teach us to be strong and not show our emotions, to keep continuing. But that gets hard after a while."

— Anonymous Facebook Post

I remember a particularly busy night in the ER—nothing unusual, just a typical two-hour wait. If you've ever had to wait that long in an ER to see a physician, especially while feeling unwell, you know it's not a pleasant experience. In the ER and throughout most of the hospital, it's clear that patients are not exactly thrilled to be there. Even the best relief can't fully ease your worries when you're unwell and in a place you'd rather avoid. You might be confronting your own mortality, anxious about paying for your care, or concerned about your job, children, or family. Perhaps you're dwelling on an uncertain future, no matter how clear the sky may be, when you gaze out of a hospital window.

Needless to say, coming to work every day to help people in a place where they really don't want to be, to serve people who are far from their best selves, that alone can drain you a bit. There are, of course, exceptions. Those exceptional patients where you will find some of the most inspirational stories and memories, where it seems the patient is the nurse and the nurse the patient; those moments are a big part of what makes being a healthcare worker so special, so beautiful. I treasure those moments.

I will never forget, for example, one quieter ER shift as a nurse; I had the joy of caring for a very dignified, stately elderly lady who was actively dying of cancer. She was in obvious discomfort, though she wouldn't complain, yet there was a certain aura of joy around her. She had just received some pain medicine, and it was too soon for another dose. Being a quiet night, I had a few extra moments to sit beside her stretcher. I could tell she wanted to talk. As I held her hand, she spoke and told me a long story of her wonderful life and the wonderful, as she described, saintly late husband she had shared this life with. She told me about her kids, growing up, her family, and how much she cherished every moment. The way she spoke, the way she smiled, and the loving energy she gave off, I remember her vividly to this day, some 25 years later. I cherished that moment. I commented that her husband was a very lucky man to have shared this life with her; she was such a beautiful soul. She wrapped her hand around mine, weak, though as tightly as she could, looked me in the eye and said, "No, son, I was the lucky one." These were her last words on this earth as she died with her hand in mine. At this moment, I knew I would become a Hospice Nurse at some point in my career. Yes, there is such a thing as a beautiful death.

Back to the busy night. Almost nobody wants to be in the ER as a patient, and you definitely don't want to be sitting in the waiting room for two hours with moaning adults and irritable children next to and around you. I really don't remember too many specifics about this night, but I do remember that there was a house fire, much as described in Chapter 1, and some other family involved. This is back when I was a newbie in the emergency room, back in my early days when I was still an emergency room technician, an impressionable young lad.

One of the awesome hero first responder teams brought us a boy from the fire who was maybe six or seven years old. This young man was not directly caught in the flames; however, he had been overcome by smoke and was "down" long enough that he was in full cardiopulmonary arrest. Many times, in this scenario, meaning a house fire, smoke, or full arrest, the patient might not even be brought to the hospital. They would more likely be pronounced dead at the scene after being worked on by the paramedics, assuming there was no positive response to their interventions. But with a person as young as this, every chance was going to be given to resuscitate this child. I have seen what would be described as miraculous results with youth resilience. This is well documented with hypothermia and drowning events in the young, for example. As our hero team in the emergency room did our best, along with the assistance of two hero nurses who came to our from our hospital's pediatric department, we gave this young man every chance, using every trick in the book we had at the time. Unfortunately, we could never get this young man to return to this realm. Sometimes, even heroes can't save the day.

A nurse in the ER was working that night whom I will call Angie. I remember Angie was not long out of school and had been training in the emergency room as a new, full-time, bright-eyed, proud, enthusiastic, newly minted, full-fledged emergency room nurse. She had been in the ER for maybe a couple of months. However, this was probably the first time Angie had to deal with this type of event, where it was her patient on the stretcher; she was the primary nurse, and her young patient had not survived. At least, that is how I remember it. When this happens, it can create a disbelieving feeling of "How could this happen? We did everything they taught us to do? How can this happen?" It creates a feeling like you've failed. You wonder what you could have done better and ask what you might have done wrong, even though the end result was inevitable at that point. I have seen this look many times since and felt this more times than I can count, but for this case, this was still relatively new to Angie and me. I guess that is why this stands out.

As I was assisting Angie with postmortem care, I looked over for a bit and realized Angie was standing next to the stretcher where the young man lay. She wasn't talking and appeared to be weeping, frozen in place. I continued with my duties, not knowing what to say and not wanting to embarrass Angie when the charge nurse came into the room. She was a very loving and supportive person and had been helping Angie with her transition into a full-fledged ER nurse. She came into the room to see how things were going, noticed Angie standing there, walked over to her, stood next to her, put her arm around her shoulder, and said something to the effect of, "I know, I understand. We can talk this out later. But for now, we just have to suck it up, Buttercup. There's lots of other patients to see." I don't know if "later" ever came.

That memory has always stuck with me. Even years later, I know the charge nurse did not mean anything bad by it. I know she probably thought she was helping Angie get through the moment and shift with the goal of helping as many people as we could, as quickly as we could, that busy night. That's what we do. That may not be the first time I've ever heard that line, "suck it up..." but it's certainly the first time it ever stuck with me, and it's been with me ever since.

Now, shifting, I am going to introduce what I call the file cabinet. For you, it may be a box, a closet, a drawer, but I call mine a file cabinet, with the words "suck it up, Buttercup" written on the side. A place where we file away all of the bad stuff and emotional baggage. Healthcare workers, first responders, police officers – we all have our file cabinet, whether in the ER, in the field after a bad car accident, literally picking up body parts off the side of the road, or after a tense domestic violence call where one person was holding a gun, intoxicated, and you are just praying your bulletproof vest works as it should if things get worse while pictures of your children flash before your eyes. Just like after a nurse dealing with a young mother who just gave birth in the ER and threw massive pulmonary emboli (blood clot) who will not be around to breastfeed her new bundle of joy or watch them grow, there's always another call waiting; there's always a next case waiting. Schools, educators, preceptors, it's rare to be able to take the time to prepare someone for how to deal with such an event. We are not trained to do that. We are taught to be strong, to move on, to "suck it up," So we take that file, put it in our file cabinet, and do just that, move on. We don't allow ourselves to admit or show weakness or vulnerability.

After a while, this file cabinet becomes quite a burden. And you can't go home later and talk to your spouse or loved one and say, "Hey, let's deal with this issue and get rid of it." How do you talk about it? How do you explain? So, the file cabinet just gets deeper and heavier. I can easily remember, and those of you in the field for a while probably can too, being a young nurse or being new to the field, at the end of a 12-hour shift, looking forward to going out with some of my coworkers, maybe having breakfast or a drink, and looking forward to working the next day. But the heavier that file cabinet gets, the less energy you seem to have, the less enthusiasm you have when you get ready for work, and every minute of every shift starts to become more taxing. These are some of the first symptoms; this is where burnout begins.

So, the first step is to recognize this and figure out where you've been storing your files. Identification of the disease is the first step toward a cure. I was able to recognize my file cabinet, realize it for what it was, and throw the whole damn thing in the trash. You, my hero friend, can do this too.

IV: Defining Burnout

"I've watched guys die almost every day. Why didn't I ever cry for them?"

— Hawkeye,
played by actor Alan Alda

"Look, all I know is what they taught me in command school. There are certain things about war. And rule number 1 is young men die. Rule number 2 is doctors can't change rule number 1."

— Henry Blake,
played by actor McLean Stevenson

M*A*S*H, S1, E17

So, what exactly is this thing we call burnout? Personally, I'm almost offended by the term. To me, the term burnout insinuates some flaw within yourself. It's almost stigmatizing to say someone is or has burned out, like a flaw or a weakness, almost a dirty word, too embarrassing to even admit. Dr. Zubin Damania, who has done many studies on this, prefers to call healthcare burnout Moral Injury. However, for the purpose of this book, I will use the common term burnout.

In defining the common term burnout, no one single definition seems to match another. Webster's Dictionary defines burnout as exhaustion of physical or emotional strength or motivation, usually as a result of prolonged stress or frustration. That comes close. But besides the occasional negative outcomes, where does the frustration come in? Yes, healthcare can be a stressful profession, with lots of needs to satisfy seemingly at once, but more often than not, this is one of the most rewarding jobs there are.

The Mayo Clinic defines burnout as work-related stress, physical or emotional exhaustion that also involves a sense of reduced accomplishment and loss of personal identity. I think it's pretty hard to argue that in healthcare or as a first responder, we have a reduced sense of accomplishment or personal identity.

The World Health Organization, in my observations, does the best job defining burnout as a syndrome conceptualized as resulting from chronic workplace stress that has not been successfully managed. Everybody seems to have their own definition.

There are almost as many definitions for burnout as there are people making definitions. The only consistencies, it seems, are related to stress and satisfaction. Healthcare, first responder, and police work are undoubtedly stressful, but many times are highly rewarding. Working in any customer service profession is stressful; working in a factory, as a CEO, in a restaurant, as an entrepreneur or countless other professions is stressful, but the pain, disease, and life-and-death part is most unique to us heroes. We experience both extreme emotional highs and extreme lows. We must highlight the highs, be thankful, and deal with and release the lows.

Consequences of burnout, or more appropriately, moral injury, are not processed and are far-reaching, starting first with the emotional and, over time, manifesting in the physical. Depending on individual learned coping mechanisms, this affects different people in different ways, but one thing is clear: emotional stress not addressed over time will affect you both spiritually and physically. It is rare for an individual to do this naturally. I am certainly not saying that without action, you will have a complete breakdown and end up like Tom in Chapter 1. His was extreme, though more common than most would like to admit. Tom was a master of denial. We will all likely have some negative effects in our lives without heeding this call to action. Between his military experiences and long-term exposure to some of the most heart-wrenching scenes a hospital nurse can expose themselves to, Tom had a file cabinet larger and heavier than most. Tom's experiences would be more along the lines of our hero police officers and first responders, who take a brutal scene in the field and put them in as pretty a package as they can before bringing them to the hospital. I will say, however, that not properly dealing with the stress, filling up the file cabinet over time, will show its insidious results while not just taking an emotional toll, but long-term emotional repression and stress will lead to physical changes as well. This has been proven many times.

Some of the more common side effects of long-term stress and repression are localized pain, such as back, shoulder, or neck pain, fatigue, insomnia, sadness, anger, irritability, alcohol or substance abuse, heart disease, hypertension, type II diabetes, and a compromised immune system. These are all physical results that can be a result of the long-term stress of burnout, as reported and observed and reported by the Mayo Clinic. Also, going through burnout, you eventually find it hard to relate to the "normal world" with their "normal problems." You may find it hard to be able to relate to anyone who hasn't had the same experiences as you. You will see the world around you differently, and those who have not experienced this probably cannot relate. It is very rare for any healthcare worker or first responder to maintain a relationship with, for example, a business executive, CEO, or banker. They exist in different worlds.

When you don't confront and dissolve your file cabinet, you are likely to lose yourself, your empathy, your compassion, and the very beautiful part of you that brought you to these professions in the first place. The only people I have observed who have been able to sustain naturally are those who are truly able to own and hold onto the joyful experiences, creating a balance between the light and the dark. Or they instinctively know how not to hold on to the pain. These heroes are very, very rare. Most of us, over time, become overwhelmed with the dark. We build shells or walls between ourselves and the rest of the world for protection, and we find ourselves withdrawing, tending toward social avoidance and/or bad habits. We have difficulty relating to others.

So, what's the answer? Do you just quit? Avoid these professions altogether? Do something else, quitting what you so passionately strived for, giving up on the hero within you, the joy, the ecstasy that cannot be found easily outside of this profession? Give up your calling, the true inner you? I find this to be sad, like a life not wholly lived.

So you may ask, what can I do? I have been shown a way to do this, the way to hold on to the passion that brought you here, a way to survive and thrive as a healthcare worker and first responder, and in the following chapters, through experiences and observations, I will show you how you too can do your best to put everything into perspective, how to not let your empathy and compassion take the best of you, how to practice what is called mindfulness, how to be present, releasing the dark while holding onto the joy.

To begin, start by focussing on being thankful for the joyful outcomes while realizing that even for the most emotionally charged negative outcomes, we, as a team, did the best we could with what we had at the time.

Keep perspective. Know you cannot save the world. As is said, the world may not want to be saved as we define it. Get rid of your file cabinet and deal with the difficult outcomes as they present themselves. People die, sometimes tragically. People suffer. It is a part of life. If this were not true, the world would not need the hero. Suffering occurs, and you, the hero, will bear witness. And miracles happen every day. Of this, too, you will bear witness. Negative outcomes in life-and-death situations are inevitable, as are miracles. Mindfulness, maintaining perspective, not losing yourself in your compassion, meditation rituals, prayer, yoga, identifying and releasing your file cabinet, identifying and releasing judgment: these are techniques that do work. Being present, which means releasing the past as well as future expectations, living the moment, holding onto and being thankful for the light, and knowing how and when to release the dark, are the keys.

Strive to be present.

With practice, releasing the dark is not as hard as it seems, while being thankful for the light is much more powerful than it sounds. Many studies show how powerful a force in your life thankfulness and gratitude can be. One of the great healers of our day, Oprah Winfrey, built an entire career based on being grateful. This can be found in every major religion. The University of California at Berkley's The Greater Good Science Center, a leader in research on the science of emotional and social well-being, describes gratitude as a "social glue." The keys to building strong relationships, not just relationships with others but with self, include not being too shy to pat yourself on the back, you humble hero. By practicing meditation, thankfulness, and perhaps prayer, through whatever ritual you find solace, there is an answer for you. There are many programs and systems out there. You must find which one works best for you. The system I use and will speak of in later chapters focuses on perspective, gratitude, and mindfulness, or being present. These will work within the framework of any religious belief.

Whatever you choose, you must be vigilant. Recognition and then maintaining perspective are huge first steps on this journey. Along with mindfulness, these are powerful tools and the main focus of this book.

I wish I had a magic pill or word to gift you to help you along your journey, to help you hold onto the joy that drew you to being the hero in the first place. This requires work and discipline, but it will quickly become a habit through practice. However, it is not nearly the level of work and discipline that has gotten you here in the first place, and it can save you a lot of heartache.

This, my hero friend, is what they don't teach you in school.

V: Perspectives

"Reject the sense of injury, and the injury itself disappears."

— Marcus Aurelius

Perspectives

Words create thoughts. Thoughts create feelings. Feelings create experiences. Experience creates reality.

Your word, to others and yourself, is magic. Your word to others signifies your intent, defines your purpose, and creates your experienced reality. If you allow them, the words of others can alter your reality. There was once a guy in Germany who used nothing other than words to convince one of the most highly developed and educated societies in the world at the time to alter world history from a place of hatred and fear. There are many examples of this. Words manifest. They matter.

Words, both to self and others, are what we accept and reject, what shape perception, and what creates a feeling, associate the experience, and then shapes our perceived reality. We must choose our words carefully. We must ask ourselves, "Are the words I am hearing coming from a place of love? Fear? What do we accept as our reality? Where is the word being spoken to me coming from?"

Remember, what others say, especially when coming from a place of fear and stress, does not have to reflect or become our experience. They are expressing their reality. When we bring others' thoughts and feelings into our experience, we bring into our existence their reality. This does not have to be.

If you are coming into or are in the healthcare field or that of a first responder, and you are very sensitive to or take personally the insults and cursing of strangers, you either must recognize and change that right now or choose another field. I would argue, however, that life is full of such experiences. It's just magnified when you come from a place of empathy and compassion and encounter others from a place of fear, insecurity, or suffering. You will be called everything from a guardian angel to the devil incarnate. Thick skin helps.

For those who are able to give up a level of control in their lives and put faith in those trying to help them, you will be seen and treated as their salvation, their life raft when they are drowning. In 2022, nurses were once again ranked as the most trusted profession in the United States, with 79% of those who responded saying nurses had high or very high rates of honesty and ethical standards *(Gallup)*.

Then there is the other 21%. Those who don't trust you and, as a result may treat you unkindly. For those who are ill or injured and are not able to accept loss of control, who do not deal rationally with stress, you will be viewed with fear as the embodiment of that loss of control. These individual's reality will come from a place of fear, and they will be taking out on you their fears. They will blame you for their lack of control; for now, they perceive that you are in control. This is part of what I mean by perspective. A feeling is conveyed when a word is spoken, so ask yourself where it is coming from. A place of fear? If you do not do this, their reality can become part of yours, and their words can shape your reality. You may feel hurt, angry, resentful, defensive, or all of these.

People don't always think or act logically under severe stress, and you must remember this. To most, you are an angel, and these people are able to accept that you are there to help them improve their lives. They know they are not in control. To others, you are the embodiment of pure evil because you represent that they are vulnerable, that they, in this moment, are not in control of their own lives. We tend to humbly brush off the angel compliments, for it's hard sometimes to accept that we are the hero. Our very nature tends to be that of humble servant. That is part of our nature that brought us here in the first place. We tend to brush off the concept, thoughts, and words, thus feeling that we are the hero. But we oftentimes are unable to brush off the insults completely, the words that come from their experience of pain and fear. We can end up resenting these patients who are feeling the loss of control. However, these we tend to add to the "suck it up, Buttercup" file cabinet.

Take pride in the compliments. They are from the heart. Accept that you, yes, you, are a hero. You have forsaken the chance at a more lucrative career and chosen to serve others. By these very choices, you are a hero. To some, you will represent a loss of control, a personification of their deepest fears. This is simply their reality. Do not make this yours.

When dealing with stress, disease, emotional or substance abuse issues, and possibly withdrawal, most people are simply not capable of being themselves. They don't want to be there in the hospital. It's a bill they know they can't afford. The food is often sub-par or not what you are used to (sorry, kitchen workers, we all know you do your best with what you are given). The patient experience, environment, constant noises, and smells are not their chosen surroundings. If you were ever yourself a patient, other than possibly during a time of joy, such as the birth of a newborn, you will see just how stressful this can be. Loss of independence, uncomfortable beds, noise, strange environment, hospital smells, being woken up to take a pill or get a blood pressure, can't eat what you want when you want, no freedom.... I could go on. The environment encourages stress during a person's greatest fear and vulnerability.

Judgment

Judgment is another perspective all heroes must deal with. Whether we like to admit it or not, we, as humans, constantly judge. We judge everyone we meet and see, and most harshly, we constantly judge ourselves. If you haven't yet, I strongly suggest you read "The Four Agreements." Don Miguel Ruiz dives into this much more deeply and efficiently than I have the space or power to do. But with this book, we recognize that we judge others based on our values and life choices as we have accepted into our lives and compare what we value to the lives of others. We can't necessarily understand why others make their life choices; judgment comes with that.

People know that when you enter a room, you are judging them. No matter how hard we try to hide it, it shows. This also causes people to judge themselves, for they read that judgment from you and may hate themselves for it or just resent you. And guess what: they will most likely take out this frustration on you. So, especially in healthcare, you must leave all judgment at the door, both of others and yourself. When you do this, you start to realize that this is their reality, not yours, and that's okay. You don't have to live their lives; they probably don't care to try to live as you think they "should."

Accept that their choices and beliefs, while they may not be what you would choose or believe you would make for your life, are their choices and beliefs. This is what forms their reality. Their view of the world and what is real is probably not the same as yours. And that's OK. You are the director of your movie, and they are the director of theirs. Different characters, different plots, different goals. Yours is right for you; theirs is right for them. Know this, and I mean really know this, and the file cabinet gets a little lighter. A Native American proverb usually comes to my mind. "*Never judge another until you have walked a mile in his moccasins.*" Perspectives.

VI: Compassion—Your Best Friend, Your Worst Enemy

"You were born with a voice, so open up and speak your mind, Raise consciousness and elevate how we all relate, don't hesitate, No need to be better or smarter than anybody else, Leave judgment at the door, for others and yourself."

— From the song "Revolution"
Written by Erika Wennerstrom,
Performed by "Heartless Bastards"

Compassion

Is this not largely what brought you here in the first place? The fuel that feeds the fire that burns within you? In large part, what drove you to become a police officer, first responder, and healthcare worker?

Merriam-Webster's Dictionary defines compassion as the "sympathetic consciousness of others" distress together with the desire to alleviate it." The Latin root for the word compassion is patient, which means to suffer, with the prefix com, meaning with. Compassion, originating from *compati*, literally means to suffer with (from compassion). Compassion is the connection of suffering with another person. To sometimes literally feel their emotional pain. We take on another's pain to relate, to find ways to help. We feel their pain. Since feelings become a reality, their pain becomes, on some level, our reality. This leaves a mark on us—another file in file cabinet.

Compassion is a fundamental human quality that transcends cultural and religious beliefs. It involves empathy, or the ability to understand and share the feelings of others, and sympathy, or the feeling of pity or sorrow for someone else's misfortunes. Compassion derives from a genuine desire to alleviate suffering in others. You have to almost literally take on the feelings of the other to experience compassion. In healthcare, not all stories have what we would identify as a happy ending. And we have taken that on as our own through our compassion. File cabinet?

Our compassion led us here. Only through compassion can we do our jobs. When suffering is relieved, we feel alive; we feel unlimited joy. When a child is born, when we get that passenger trapped out of the burning car unscathed, that first on-scene officer who successfully rescues and resuscitates that child who was drowning in the pool - this feeds our souls. With no other work, one gets to experience this feeling semi-regularly in one such scenario or another. We get to experience this joy almost every day! We feel it; we live the experience. We own it. We feel as if it is our own, theirs, and their loved ones' happiness, unlimited love, and joy.

So why can this feed burnout? Because despite our best efforts, not every baby is born to survive the trauma of birth (if only I would have recognized the fetal distress more quickly...) Not every passenger is successfully extracted from that car before burning alive right in front of us (if only I would have seen that passenger before tending to the driver) ...Not every resuscitation is successful (if only I would have gotten here sooner...) Sound familiar? It will. And you hear these voices and feel this pain, which can also reflect self-judgment and self-doubt.

Realize that you can only do what your training, ability, and instincts allow you to do. Would you have had ultrasound vision or the assistance of an ultrasound machine with Doppler and an experienced technician? Yeah, in an ideal situation, that child may still be alive. But you don't have ultrasound vision. There was no tech or machine available. If you could rip apart a burning car apart in an instant with your bare hands? Yeah, maybe that passenger might still be alive. But you can't. If your patrol car could maybe fly directly and avoid all those twisty roads and traffic, or if the call had just come in a little sooner, yeah, maybe you could have gotten there more quickly, and that child might still be alive. But it didn't, and you can't fly. All of this self-doubt will be going through your mind when you have to face the surviving family members and tell them their loved one did not survive. This will be going through your mind, and in some cases, potentially, for as long as you keep that file cabinet alive.

How do we keep our compassion alive? How do we keep from emotionally shutting down? Our minds are designed to protect us, to direct us away from pain and internal suffering. This is why, after a few such experiences, we feel dread at even the possibility of facing another. Sure, our training and adrenaline kick in when we get the call, but the dread our minds feed us says, do we really want to go to work today? Do we want to face this possibility again? After a while, we feel emotionally and physically drained at just the thought of going to work, where we used to approach this with such enthusiasm and full of energy. Have another glass of wine or two, drown out the voices, and deaden the pain and the self-doubt.

How do we avoid this contributor to burnout and compassion fatigue? First, pat yourself on the back, hero, and know with certainty that you did your best.

Not all stories have happy endings, despite heroic efforts. Know you tried your best. You did all you possibly could. Recognize you have your human limits. Take a moment to process this. Seek help if needed, whether from a loved one, church, coworker, or friend. Practice mindfulness. Don't be afraid to express vulnerability. Don't be afraid to speak your truth. Come up with strategies with your team that might produce more positive results in the future. Learn, don't burn, from the experience.

Providing care and support to others is admirable and heroic, but balancing your compassion for others with self-compassion and self-care is essential. I have often said as a nurse manager, "Take care of yourself first and foremost, or you cannot care for anybody." I have seen many nurses burn themselves out without regard for themselves. These nurses seem to be running full speed ahead, following their empathy and compassion with their heads down, metaphorically running with purpose, staring at the ground before them, not even seeing the brick wall in front of them.

Next, they are sprawled on the ground, unable to take another step and not realizing what happened. Burned out. (Been there.) These are what the nurse managers love because they take whatever assignments they are given with enthusiasm and accept any challenge. They are like marathon runners, running without regard for themselves.

Until they just can't. They collapse. These nurses I found as a manager are ones I need to hold back, not to take advantage of their selflessness. I would sit them down, strongly encouraging them to take some of their PTO. They need to know that the team will survive short term without them while they re-charge. You have seen or will see them. A common thread is that they all have a huge bank of unused PTO, tend to have heavier workloads than the rest, and eagerly ask for more. An observant manager will see this and "make" them take time off. We all have limits. Be aware of where yours are, and forgive yourself for your limitations.

Self-Compassion

Was there something in your past that brought you joy? Writing? Painting? Drawing? Yoga? Working out at the gym or reading a book? Maybe for you, it is exploring the world around you by hiking or riding a bike. For me, it's hiking, fishing, camping, concerts, or anything outdoors. I make a point to walk my dog twice a day and observe the beauty around me while taking time out to smell the flowers, so to speak, a twice-daily ritual, cold or hot, rain or shine, even when I am not in the mood. Whatever it is or was that brought you joy, bring this back into your life. Make it a habit. Put this on your calendar if you must. Make it so. Even when you just don't feel like doing it, force yourself. Do it. Re-spark and maintain the joy. Speak to someone, anyone, who understands the challenges you are experiencing. A therapist, coworker(s), a close friend, a lover. Admit you are not perfect, that you have human limitations, and that you are vulnerable. We all are.

Don't blame yourself for what would be referred to as negative outcomes. They are inevitable in this world.

Everyone goes through periods of suffering. All lives eventually end, some inexplicably too soon. Even the greatest hero cannot prevent this. I can't stress this enough. I know you are strong, but nobody, not even you, is that strong or as strong as you would like to think you are. You will feel relief by expressing this and admitting to yourself and others that we are all human, even you. We are all vulnerable, and this includes you. It's OK. It's part of the living human experience. Know this at a deep level, a soul level. You are only human. Accept this. Just this admission alone will help you preserve your self-love and self-compassion.

When you know this, admit this to yourself, and allow that you are "only human," you will feel relieved. Know that there is no such thing as a mistake; there are lessons on how to do things a little differently next time. In whatever you do, do the best that you can at the time, and know that you did. Only then can you truly remove your self-judgment and self-doubt by practicing self-love, self-acceptance, and self-compassion. You will regain and maintain your sense of self-love and joy. Don't be afraid to set limits. Only then can you avoid that brick wall.

Compassion.

VII: You Never Know

"Do your little bit of good where you are; it is those little bits of good put together that overwhelm the world."

— Archbishop Desmond Tutu

Patients can cause a lot of frustration in us and really challenge our views. This statement is obvious to anyone who has been a first responder or healthcare worker. For those new to or considering the field, this is another concept they don't teach you in school. From the "frequent flyer" alcoholic or drug addict to the diabetic who just can't seem to do the "right" thing to the oxygen tank-dependent COPD patient who still smokes but blames you because they can't breathe, we have all encountered these patients. This can be frustrating, and I can add another file.

Each individual is like a pebble being tossed into the ocean of the world. That pebble, or individual, has a ripple effect that spreads literally across the world, far beyond what you can see. You don't know, and they may not be able to tell you why they do what they do. But everyone has good in them. Everyone does a good deed now and then. What good deed have they yet to do? How will that good deed, like a pebble, ripple across the world? As frustrating as these individuals may seem, as taxing as it becomes to once again drag that person out of their opioid-induced bliss of near death and being cursed for doing so, then seeing them again next week, maybe this time having aspirated and being admitted to the ICU. Still, you have given them another chance to make a difference. To cause a ripple, they might not know they caused it. To change the world, perhaps. Keep in mind you never know.

Many such individuals have a moment of awakening, a rebirth we will never see. Or, they may not. But you and I don't know who these individuals may touch in this ocean of humanity in the future. They may somehow inadvertently inspire the next Einstein, the next Jonas Salk, the next Gandhi, the next Dr. Martin Luther King Jr. Honestly, you never know what ripple effect they may have. Your compassion toward them, in fact, may be the only love they experience in this world. Your compassion and the unconditional love you show may be what, upon reflection, makes them realize they are worthy of love, which can lead to self-love, which can easily change lives. They may make different choices to become successful, caring parents, aunts, or uncles. They may have an everlasting positive effect on another's life or encourage the next great writer, musician, and artist that affects millions of lives. You never know.

So before these files were added to the file cabinet, these were files that never needed to be. Just remember the pebble, the ripple, the ocean of humanity. And you never know. How many lives have I touched in my almost 40 years of healthcare? How many ripples have I helped to create? Sometimes, even the negative ripples have a positive effect, showing someone what choices not to make - a positive effect on the world through negative action. If only one in a thousand turned out to be one that helped touch the life of a present or future breakthrough scientist, innovator, inspired artist, musician, or teacher, then I really have helped in some way change the world. It's almost inevitable. I will never know, but the odds are high that with all the lives I have touched in those close to 40 years, I have. Ripples.

Another side of you never know – let me tell you about "Joe."

Joe was a very frustrating, homeless, foul-smelling alcoholic man. I will never forget old Joe. This was during one of those cold northeast winters. Sure, there were shelters, but Joe's penchant for less than poor hygiene and lack of social skills in his usual drunken state made these shelters off limits to Joe, even if he had had the desire to take advantage of one. When Joe was brought into the ER, you could be on the opposite end, with many walls in between, but it didn't take long before you knew he was here. He smelled that bad.

Joe lived in the streets. He had multiple layers of clothing on to keep him warm. He drank, then passed out, wherever, drunk-stinking drunk. Full of urine and feces, unwashed since the last ER visit, scabies and scabs... you get the picture.

Someone would find Joe on the side of the street, often passed out on the road, un-rousable. What could the police and first responders do? They couldn't take him to jail to sleep it off - to be a cellmate with Joe would be considered cruel and unusual punishment. And besides, by law, you must be first medically cleared. So the ambulance was called to take him to the ER, then there was the need to disinfect the truck afterwards, again and again, and again...

If you happened to be working at the time, and good old Joe came in, and it was your turn, your shift just went to hell. Each of us had a thick file labeled simply "Joe" in our cabinet. Full PPE (personal protective equipment), fighting to get his disgusting clothes removed, with nothing but resistance and curses from Joe, because all Joe wanted, was to be left alone. Multiple blood draws with assistance holding him still enough to find a useful vein or two, IVs, Quell coating for the scabies after fighting to clean his skin the best you could, blood cultures, and all the while, you knew in the morning, Joe would be just sober enough put back on his filthy clothes, sign out against medical advice, go back to the street, and start all over again. Even though he could not speak clearly, Joe knew his rights. So predictable, so Joe.

Even in his most lucid moments, you could not have a real conversation with Joe. He had a deep, raspy, projecting voice, and you could catch maybe every third or fourth word. I managed to ascertain that old Joe revered Winston Churchill, was lukewarm on FDR, and had nothing but unrepeatable things to say about poor Eleanor. But this all seemed along the lines of people who talk passionately about their political views today. No different.

As you might expect, Joe went too far one day, and his body just gave out. It was honestly amazing he had lasted so long. Joe came to the ER in his usual state but with one major difference. He was not fighting. He was limp and thus compliant. Joe was in severe sepsis. You knew that even if we could even get him stabilized, he was not signing out in the morning.

Due to the need for speed, with no blood pressure, Joe barely breathing, unresponsive, and a thready, barely palpable pulse, we just cut those old disgusting clothes off. We noted that his old army jacket was lined and insulated with a large amount of cash bills. Multiple IVs and drips, a breathing tube, a ventilator on the knife's edge between life and death. We somehow managed to get enough stability to get Joe to the ICU. It seemed a miracle we did. None of us thought Joe would survive, let alone leave the hospital through the front door again. Next patient.

But old Joe did manage to survive. Having been in the ICU for a couple of weeks, Joe woke up. He was sober, probably for the first time in many years. What a testament to our first responder, nurse, physician, and ancillary staff heroes. And Joe was able to talk. In semi-full sentences with some clarity and Joe realized how he had almost died. Joe, now, was scared straight.

It turned out that Joe had a living sister with whom he hadn't been in contact for "years." Through the work of our awesome social work team, they were able to contact Joe's sister, a sweet retired widow in the next state, just an hour or so away.

Though Joe was still not talkative about his past, he did say he had served in the military. This, by now, is the late 80s and early 90s, and Joe was past 70. I never figured out how someone who lived a life like that made it to his 70s. But, here he was.

Joe's sister, as far as Joe's history, was more forthcoming. It turned out that Joe was one of the most highly decorated American marines in the European theater during World War II. He was so highly regarded that he was chosen to be present, possibly one of the Pall Bearers for FDR on that day (the sister said it was true, Joe said, "She doesn't know what she is talking about.")

Regardless, Joe, the one who caused so much vitriol for so long, was actually an American Treasure, a Hero of Heroes. Joe sacrificed his entire being and soul, knowingly or not, so you and I could be free here today. I can't imagine, don't want to try to imagine, what demons were hidden in poor old Joe's file cabinet.

When Joe was finally wheeled out of the hospital to go live with his now reunited sister, who was sparkling clean and smelling good, toothlessly smiling ear to ear from the pictures... I happened to be off that day. He asked to be taken to the ER, where I was told he gave a very emotional brief thank you to the entire staff and an apology for past actions. It's not a dry eye in the department, even for me, as I write this now, and I was off that day.

You never know...

VIII: Background, Healing

"Every religion is the product of the conceptual mind trying to explain the mystery."

— Ram Dass

Recognition or one might say diagnosis, of any disease is an essential first step toward avoidance or recovery. We have to know what we are fighting or guarding against. The next essential step is to prepare, choose the correct armor, and choose an appropriate cure. In the fight against burnout, your next steps are to recognize where the "enemy" lies and how to fight back.

With burnout, the "enemy" lies within, represented in my mind by the "suck it up, Buttercup" example as a cabinet full of files. For you, you can identify this however you like. The important part is not how you visualize this but the recognition that it exists and how unattended this "fire within" affects you and your daily life. This "fire within" will smolder, like a campfire left not completely extinguished overnight, like embers leading to "burnout." Fuel for the fire is your file cabinet; carnage is your compassion, joy, energy, and ability to live in a carefree way instead of implementing self-destructive habits or avoidance. So, where is the extinguisher of this destructive flame? What tools can we use to douse this insidious disease that leaves our empathy in ashes?

Psychologists such as Sigmund Freud devoted much research and energy to this. Freud defined this as an example of the unconscious mind, supporting the preconscious rather than the conscious. According to Freud, the unconscious mind is a reservoir of feelings, thoughts, urges, and memories outside of our conscious awareness. The unconscious contains contents that may be unacceptable or unpleasant, such as feelings of pain, anxiety, or conflict.

There are many studies delving into our levels of awareness or our conscious minds. This research helps us understand how and why we react, our levels of awareness, and, thus, our reactions to what we are experiencing. How we react, why we feel the way we do toward what we are perceiving - you can spend an entire career studying just that. As discussed, there are three levels according to Freud, seven according to Carl Jung, and many in between according to which study you choose. Without delving too deeply into our levels of awareness or consciousness, it is safe to say that all psychologists would agree our experiences, feelings, reactions, and related decisions go much deeper than simply conscious awareness and resultant feelings and decisions. Politicians, advertisers, and all forms of media exist, thrive, and compete within these realms. Suffice it to say for this book and in discussing burnout, and we must go to where the embers burn. We must go within.

The following chapters go on. I cannot tell you what is best for you; I can only tell you what has and does work for me and those I have shown this to. There is no right or wrong way to fight this flame. It is safe to say, however, the first step is to recognize the flame and where it burns. Once we recognize the flame, the next step is to get rid of it and block the fire's fuel so it can never flare up again. The next steps are up to you, my hero.

Where I am coming from...

I was not raised in what would be called a traditional religious sphere. While we sporadically attended some Christian church services, these were not routine. Though I remember a warm feeling in these environments, they were not regular enough to become ingrained. I never attended a Bible study class, for example. I could not even tell you what denomination these few services I attended were labeled. And though we celebrated traditional Christian holidays, these were more family-focused gatherings than celebrations based on the religious meaning behind them. Regarding beliefs, I was blessed to be able to attend a Quaker school; this is where I found my perspectives.

When I had questions about tradition and what spiritual road map I would choose, I looked to those around me. My classmates. Now, many may argue my conclusions, which is fine. This is to show you what I concluded and how I got my perspectives. Remember, this is based on a small child's perception starting at age six. Also remember, I am not here to tell you what is right or what is wrong for you or which religion is the true path. Each religion is a true path. Whichever system fits you, when you commit yourself, the results will be the same. You can rediscover or maintain inner peace and harmony. I certainly am not saying you must become a Quaker.

Quakerism, for those who do not know, is not a church by any traditional means. It is far easier to describe a Quaker than to define Quakerism. I, as a small child, found myself attending this school with other children of a variety of traditional religious backgrounds – Christian, Jewish, Agnostic, and Atheist.

It didn't matter. These were all, like me, budding little Quakers. I asked myself, being too shy to seek advice, how could this be?

Quakers, while its founder was based in Christianity, is otherwise described as "The Society of Friends" and does not have a traditional building that is what is commonly called a church. We had "Meeting Houses." Quakers, though we do recognize elders, do not have a spiritual hierarchy; instead, we are encouraged to "go within" or develop our own relationship with "God," "the Great Spirit," "Yaweh," whatever term you would use. Develop your own relationship "within you" and the "higher power" to seek the inner spirit relationship between you and "God," "Allah," "the Almighty," "Deity," or "the Great Spirit." Quakers generally believe that there is that which some call God within each of us, though no definition of "God" is ever really given.

Common threads in Quakerism are integrity, equality, simplicity, community, stewardship of the earth, and peace. Many movements in America's younger days were born of Quakerism at a time in

America when Quakers were more prominent. Pennsylvania, "The Quaker State," is exemplified by William Penn, a devout Quaker. It is the home to the first capital of the US, York, Pennsylvania, and third, Philadelphia, where the Declaration of Independence and Constitution were conceived and debated, and whose motto was and still is "The City of Brotherly Love". Though not exclusive to Quakerism, this is an expression of the Quaker ideal. Philadelphia was considered the main terminus in later years for the Underground Railroad for escaped slaves, for example. Many of the original women's equality movements in the late 1800s and early 1900s were Quakers. "Do unto others as you would have others do unto you," known as The Golden Rule, was a strong sentiment that was and is still the thread of my early "religious" training. Quakerism has no religious hierarchies, pastors, priests or the like.

So, when I looked for dogmatic references, I recognized that, from my perspective as a young child, all of my classmates were good people. No matter their traditions, no one was better or more worthy than the next. So, how could I, from this perspective, choose one traditional religion over another? How could I take the point of view that this doctrine is the "correct" path, whereas that one is the "incorrect" path? Mine is right, so yours must be wrong. I am not saying this is what all religions believe; this was just from the perspective of a 6-year-old child. I saw this as simply your path; no one path or person was inherently "better" than the other.

If all people had this perspective, that my group perspective is my group perspective, yours is yours, and no one is inherently right or wrong, I would argue this world would have a completely different experience.

Either way, this book is not meant to be preachy or to espouse Quakerism; it just helps going forward to explain where I am coming from and how I arrived here. From where I stand, again, there is no right way.

Quaker meetings involve extended "moments of silence." These would last about 30 minutes, and you were encouraged to go within. No real direction given, no traditional preaching, no direct guidance. It is not easy to achieve silence with so many young, fidgety children. But they manage. I used this time of self-exploration to ponder these ideas of different religious doctrines, not through extensive study but rather for basic threads of commonality, the origin of all. This led me to read such authors as Richard Bach's Jonathan Livingston Seagull and Illusions, the later Joseph Campbell's Power of Myth series, and Karen Armstrong's A History of God over time. Then, when I was older, I saw Neale Donald Walsh and his Conversations with God series. There were many others. My young mind perceived that all these great religions must have some common source, and that is what I was searching for. All had seemed to have a common thread: The Golden Rule.

I perceived that since there were so many differences in how "reality" was presented, my personal conclusion was that whatever the "ultimate" reality is, it must be beyond our human minds and language to explain or clearly perceive, or else we would all agree.

If true reality was ours to know, there would not be so many different religions. Right or wrong, I concluded that each religion was developed to explain in understandable terms and traditions that which cannot otherwise be explained or commonly understood. I wanted to know and understand their roots. That which could not commonly be understood. The root of it all. That was and remains my inner-stated goal.

So these 30-minute weekly periods of silence would lead me to a sort of trance, which, at the time, my small mind referred to as "self-hypnosis." I really enjoyed this state. I can even remember reading a book on self-hypnosis techniques and how to achieve this. I started practicing this in my room at night, using a candle in the dark to achieve what I now realize was focus and mindfulness, though, at the time, I would not have used these terms. And what I thought was self-hypnosis, really, was just what is now and then commonly called meditation, or "being present".

So, the rest of this book on burnout uses this perspective as its root. This non-denominational perspective of commonality of experience. Mindfulness, being present, meditation, and energy.

IX: Mindfulness, Being Present

"If you were conscious, that is to say totally present in the Now; all negativity would dissolve almost instantly. It could not survive in your presence."

— Eckhart Tolle

Being present has a double meaning. There is being present, as in attendance, being physically here. The spiritual meaning, what is also referred to as mindfulness, refers to being aware of nothing but the here and now, a moment in time.

All the world's religions recommend this in one way or another, through teaching and/or practice, living in the moment with full awareness. Whether it is the Muslim call to prayer, the Christian moment of silence, or Zen Buddhism's "Nowness" and meditations. Jewish, Taoist, Hindu, and Native American practices, in one way or another, all religions encourage some sort of a Carpe Diem or seize the day approach to life. Appreciate the moment, the beauty and the love around us; this present moment will not come to us again. With this moment, be thankful. Always remember the golden rule.

Our more natural state of mind is to live with an eye on the past, which reflects by association what we look forward to in the future with either fear or longing. With this, we make judgments on what we are to or might encounter, be it rational, logical, or even truly relational.

A personal example is that I have since I can remember, a fear of heights. I have beaten the worst of this, but even the second or third step of a ladder for most of my years gave me extreme anxiety. Was I inadvertently dropped as a child? Did I fall out of my crib, climbing over the rail? Fall out of bed? I will never know. But my mind's reaction, and since mind-filtered awareness is designed to protect me, has always associated heights with an extremely emotional and, thus, physical response, even to the idea of heights. Were you frightened as a child by a snake? A spider that crawled on you? It sticks with you. Whatever, you have probably experienced the same unreasonable and illogical reaction with this or some other stimuli.

The best way to beat this is to let go of the past and not focus on a possible future. To be present.

In healthcare, we make many such associations over time, then all the time. This is especially true in any situation where we doubt or blame ourselves on some level for what we experienced as a negative outcome. We value life. We trust our training and ability to protect and preserve life. We all, on some level, say that, yes, people die. But in practice, on a deeper level, we don't want to accept this. Death of our patient we view as a failure, particularly when it is someone young. These experiences also can make us ponder the fragility of our own lives. They, from our minds' eyes, are not supposed to die. This is also how we are trained to think. This is why hospice was invented; general medicine does not know how to deal with this systematically and intuitively. Death undesirable outcomes, these leave a mark. Enough of these, if not dealt with, not put into perspective, with associated self-doubt and judgment, and our file cabinets are now plural and overflowing.

We must, must learn to be present. To put everything in perspective. With this, we will stop associating the past with the present. Release the past from this moment. Don't associate these unwanted feelings with possible outcomes in the future. Be present. Simply said, it works.

The best way, no matter your spiritual beliefs, is to take just thirty seconds before and after each event, tune out everything around you, close your eyes, take a deep breath, paying attention to nothing but the breath, and as you breathe out, say to yourself, "Be Present". Do this three times if you can. Take longer breaths if you have time. You will be amazed at how you feel.

Ask any artist, musician, scientist, or writer what it means to be present, or some would say "in the zone". How do you feel after deep, focused prayer with no distractions? After focused meditation, yoga, hiking, and being aware of nature, athletes such as marathon runners also know this level of focus. There are too many examples to list. If you think about it, you have experienced this feeling. Mindfulness means being in the zone, being present, and having no external distractions.

Our society is full of forms of distractions vying for our attention. Cell phones, television, advertisement and marketing are everywhere, as well as social media and 24-hour news. Most are designed on some level to create outrage and fear. Fear and outrage hold our attention longer than a story about a boring, loving life or harmony. We barely make it through those headlines. Or at least it doesn't hold us as long, with as much attention. Politicians and the media know this. Outrage works.

You can practice this in your daily life. Try it. You will be amazed at how you feel. Be present in whatever you do. When I realized how transformative this was, I started setting the timer on my phone, first every 90 minutes, then a few days later 75, then 60. When the timer went off, I was reminded to say to myself, if even briefly, to breathe, to "be present." I looked at my phone and looked forward to my next reminder. It feels so liberating. Do this, and it starts to become a habit. What file cabinet?

You will start to remind yourself when you wake up in the morning. When starting your car, when drinking your coffee, tea, smoothie, or whatever your morning ritual is, take a moment. As you take this further, your judgment of yourself and others starts to fade away. It must. You are losing past associations and future expectations. Mindfulness. Being present.

X : Energy

"If you want to find the secrets of the universe, think in terms of energy, Frequency and vibration."

— Nikolai Tesla

We are all made up of energy. You can call this energy life force, universal energy, nature energy, holy spirit, whatever fits your belief system; its existence is truth. When we are alive, there is something there that is no longer there when we die. It doesn't matter what you believe this energy is. Souls, spirit, whatever. It is simply no longer present in what we call our body.

All people give off energy. All humans project their energy. You know this when you think of that person who, when they enter a room, they immediately become a person who seems to "light up the room."

People are drawn to them. Their presence is almost omnipresent. You feel better because they are there, even though you personally may not know them. This is because of the energy they project. They are what we would commonly call outgoing, warm personalities. What this all refers to is energy. They are projecting their loving energy. Their energy is actually going out into the room. They might otherwise be anonymous. But you are aware of their presence. Some might even refer to this as they have a strong aura, an energy term. At least on some level, they have drawn your attention. Others may enter the room, and you barely notice them, if at all. We may say shy, introverted, or humble observers. We have all experienced this.

Why is that? You might say, for example, that this is due to fame. I would counter it's partly their energy that helped bring them fame. We all have some talent. They have chosen to focus on their talents, fine-tune them, and, without fear of rejection, project their energy. The people who project their energy are the ones who draw our attention, for better or worse. We call them extroverts. We might call them magnetic or repulsive personalities. Magnetic and repulsive are both energy terms.

Most people are afraid to project their energy. This fear could be cultural, meaning they are trained to believe that being humble is the more honorable path. It could be that they have been judged in their lives and now are practicing an ongoing self-judgment and feel they are not worthy of attention. They might convince themselves that they've been told they have no talents to offer, and so they begin to see themselves that way. This self-perception influences how they present themselves and shapes their experiences. Any way you look at it, they are holding their energy back, doing their best not to draw attention. So, this is how others react to them– by politely ignoring them.

A basic rule of energy is that the energy you choose to project is the energy you will receive. Yes, this can be a choice like energies attract. This is true, a basic rule of energy. If you come from a place of fear, for example, or see the world as a dangerous place to be feared, you will project your fear and receive fearful stimuli to reinforce it. You may push people away, even those you love most, to reinforce a need for protection from the insecurity of love. Others will feel that energy and be afraid of you.

If you see the world as a loving and happy place and want to be loved and joyful, loving people will feel the love you project and be attracted to you as long as they believe they are worthy of that love. The persons who reject your happiness and joyful energy are generally the people who themselves reject the idea that the world is a happy and joyful place. They will be "turned off" by you. The people who are attracted to you seek to reinforce their views of what life can be: a world full of joy and happiness. They see themselves as worthy of receiving this gift from you. Your loving energy.

We all know this on some intuitive level. I am just trying to help you visualize this and put it into words. You project the energy you allow yourself or choose to project or receive. This is true because you can actually choose, or intend, whatever energy you choose if you are mindful of the present.

If you come from a place of fear, or you are afraid of rejection, you will hold your energy back to avoid what you see as judgment. This is because you have been taught to judge yourself constantly. If you have no fear of judgment, you are more likely to project your energy, judgment be damned, because you know you are a being of love and that you are worthy (you are). If you have been taught to fear judgment and constantly judge yourself, you will instinctively hold back your energy, hoping nobody tries to enter your energy zone.

If you have been taught to, or if you have chosen to, love yourself unconditionally, you will project this without fear of judgment.

So, what does all this energy talk have to do with healthcare and burnout?

In terms of energy, we must understand that energies attract– we must recognize when entering into any relationship... be it in our personal lives, the patient-provider relationship, with our neighbors, the grocery, clerk, or any other context. The love of self projects love while the judgment of self projects judgment. When people sense they are being judged, they usually don't like that feeling. These are sometimes hard-to-swallow truths. This is a projection. This is the truth.

Now, when you enter a casual or otherwise relationship with empathy or compassion, this is another truth altogether. You are trying to understand where a person is and their feelings, so you enter as a sponge. This is where healthcare workers usually are. When you do this, you are an empathetic person; you are sensitive and absorb the energy of the person, taking it on as if it were your own. You know what I am talking about if you have been this person. If you are around a depressed person, you feel their depression as if it were your own. Remember, feelings create reality. You become fearful or loving if you come around a fearful or loving person. The empathetic person becomes like a chameleon. Most people who choose healthcare are strongly empathetic. Think of the states of emotion most patients are in. We take this on. We literally "feel their pain" and then move on to the next patient. File cabinet?

How can we avoid this cycle? How can we escape this and save ourselves while helping others?

The answer is intent. You can change the energy you project and, thus, the energy you receive. Remember, only like energies, when projected, can attract. This basic rule of energy is a universal truth.

So to do this, my Hero friend, you:

- Become present by practicing mindfulness
- Say to yourself, before entering the room or encounter, I will intend love, healthy energy, and joy.
- Believe it. Become it. Try it, I dare you.

It works.

All people just want to receive love. Be the source. Intend to project love and joy; love and joy are all you will receive. This is true, even in dire life-death situations. Leave judgment behind you, both of yourself and others. Decide "I am present, and I intend unconditional love and joy", and mean it. Then, enter the room. Even in the most dire of circumstances, you will make the other feel better, and you will feel better yourself for what you receive. You can totally change your energy and the energy of your room. You become the source. What file cabinet? The key is to be present, truly feel it, truly go to the deepest part of your being, and mean it.

Intend.

You may think this all sounds kind of outlandish, but you will see it is absolutely true. You will start to look forward to patient encounters again over time because you will receive what you project. Love. Joy. Even in the harshest of cases. Don't feel sorry for them; feel joy in their presence. They will feel more joyful just because you are there, because of the love you bring.

The more you practice this along with mindfulness, the more this will just become a habit. You will feel the change within you when you stick with it. This is true in all situations of your life. I used to be shy, introverted, and avoidant. Since I have learned this, I am open, if not extroverted, "naked" on the stage. Heck, I'm even writing a book. I look forward to all encounters for the love I am bound to receive, where I used to avoid encounters. Who would have thought? Not anyone who knew me before I learned this, I have heard so many times, Keith, you have changed. I am now unafraid of the criticisms and judgment I will surely receive from some after baring my soul inner self here, and before that would have kept me from trying. But that's not who I am now. I am present or constantly returning to the present... At one time, I feared the present, but now I am like a child on their birthday, joyfully opening the moment that was present to me, my present! My intent is love, to help others excel and feel joy. So I fear no judgment...

Intent...

XI: Other Stuff

"...be at peace with God, whatever you conceive Him to be. Whatever your labors and aspirations, in the noisy confusion of life, keep peace in your soul. With all its sham, drudgery and broken dreams, it is still a beautiful world. Be cheerful. Strive to be happy."

— Max Ehrman from Desiderata

There are, as you know or will see, other causes of burnout. In this book, the main focus is on areas within your control. The COVID pandemic, for example, was an aberration causing a unique and extreme cause for burnout. However, as this type of global event has thus far been once every hundred years, I will not attempt to address it here.

Another factor of burnout that you can control I would call your appetite. Many Healthcare workers fall into the common modern-day trap of desiring more than they can afford. If you are like most Americans, you spend around 105% of what you earn annually and have negligible savings. This leads you to the desire to work more and get that overtime, but instead of saving more, you spend more. I have done this for years. Over time, you may come to realize there is no "stuff" that will bring you joy more than peace of mind, a cushion in the bank, and being present. If you are constantly worried about bills or buying the next great car, phone, a bigger house, or whatever, you will never truly find ease from stress; you will not be present.

Healthcare workers generally work 36 hours per week, three twelve-hour shifts, sometimes seven shifts over two weeks. That's enough. You will never find a working HC worker on the bread line. If a job requires more or mandates overtime, I would argue that the job is probably not for you, should you choose to live a better life. Working more, especially in healthcare, constantly seeking that extra in your check for whatever you think will bring you joy, seeking that elusive unicorn of happiness outside the self, is a surefire path to burnout. Find a side hustle if you have the energy and drive. Something you really enjoy. You never know.

Yes, the inherent stressors of the profession are there. Between regulation, charting, focus, and so on, these are hardly isolated to healthcare. We do not need to work two full-time low-wage jobs to support our children unless we simply have an appetite bigger than our means. We do not have a competitive sales quota to meet just to keep our jobs and get paid. We can take vacations without worrying about who is watching the store. We actually have it, and on the whole, it's really good.

If you find there is no money at the end of the week, or you have ongoing consumer debt that cannot be cleared monthly beyond a possible car payment and mortgage, seek a financial counselor. It's OK to acknowledge you need this help. Our society is a consumer society; many pressures you don't even realize encourage you to spend more, creating a perceived need. Create and follow a plan. As stated, there is nothing that can make you feel more free, reassured, and joyful financially than the feeling of a cushion of money in the bank. Staffing is another omnipresent issue in healthcare. A big part of the reason for this is burnout.

This book, or similar, should be a must-read for all those entering or working the field. What they don't teach you in school. Addressing and curbing burnout alone and allowing yourself to experience the joy you sought when you entered this profession will help with much of your staffing woes. Burnout creates a vicious cycle of staffing issues. Know your limits. Set your boundaries. Don't allow your management system to take advantage of your desire to serve by giving you a larger load than you can reasonably manage. Is this selfish? Yes, it's taking care of yourself. Never feel guilty for putting yourself and your family first. If your facility consistently insists that you take that extra load beyond common accepted standard, subtly remind them there are more jobs than workers. You will have no problem finding a more fitting environment for you. Stand your ground; stand up for yourself.

Healthcare workers, in general, aren't great at this. They often focus on addressing needs and want to fulfill them. However, it's crucial to remember that you can't sustain either your effectiveness or your well-being over time if you don't prioritize self-care before patient care. Frustration with management is a common issue as well. As per above, know that management cannot give you more than you are willing to accept. You are a licensed professional. You've worked hard to be here. You have options. Though it may seem that management does not care about you or the patients, on the whole, this is not true. If it is true, then the very viability of the facility or management system is in serious jeopardy. In this age of instant reviews, competition for business and staff, and social media, you cannot survive as a business without paying attention to your customers and your staff. Do not be afraid to, with respect, speak your mind. If you let your frustrations build, you will either begin to hate going to work or let your frustrations be known in a less-than-productive way. Speak your mind; let your voice be heard. Management will listen, or they will not be long for that role.

At the same time, you do need to have some view of the management side. Healthcare is, after all, a business. As such, in the face of constantly rising costs and litigation, the business bills also need to be met, or there will be no jobs. Paychecks will bounce. Services will be compromised. Cuts will need to be made to keep the doors open. Be sensitive to this. Try to be as frugal as possible without compromising patient care. Your managers are people, too. They also make mistakes. Allow for this, but don't be afraid to speak your mind again in a respectful way. Managers deserve to be respected just as you do. Remember the golden rule.

Everybody wants more pay. The highest-paid executive? They probably would not turn down a raise.

As stated, healthcare will not make you rich and will not bring you fame, but it will not leave you hungry. The market is what the market is. If you really believe you are undervalued for your skills and time compared to current market value, then speak to your manager about this, tell them you are going to or are currently looking at other opportunities and mean it. If the market shows that you are underpaid, you will easily find other choices. There are more jobs in almost every market than qualified workers, and with the aging population, this is only going to be amplified.

Aside from extreme situations like a global pandemic or war, burnout in healthcare can be avoided and overcome. Remember, you can choose not to be a victim. Joy can be preserved. Few professions—aside from teachers, research scientists, and political leaders—have as profound an impact on the world and a lasting ripple effect on people and society as healthcare workers do.

You are my friend, a Hero.

Final Chapter: The Voice Within

"The two most important days in your life are the day you are born and the day you figure out why."

— Mark Twain

"It is through science that we prove, but it is through intuition that we discover."

— Henri Poincaré

As you progress in your healthcare career, you develop and find what I will call an inner voice. We all have one, not just healthcare workers, but in repeated life-and-death scenarios, it can become more acute. This is the voice of intuition, gut instinct, however you choose to identify it. This may be an actual voice or come to you as a feeling. Partly, it is a voice coming from an association from similar cases in the past mixed with training, a sort of association, and partly from a place we can't really identify. Call it the heart. We all have it, but it becomes clearer and more identifiable the longer you are in your role and the more confident you get with your skills. Learn to trust this voice.

I remember this one case almost as if it were yesterday. I came on shift in the ER one night, later in my ER career, while living in the sunshine state. It was a busy day; I was working the night shift. We got a call that a young 30-something female was being brought in in full cardiac arrest. She has no known medical history; she suffered a sudden arrest while exercising. She had already been down in the field for 40 minutes as the paramedics on the scene did their best to revive her with no result.

She arrived on a stretcher, was transferred to an ER stretcher, and was met by the ER physician, respiratory therapist, X-ray technician, EKG technician, and several other ER staff, including an additional nurse, to assist with documentation and manage the code cart. We were informed that her husband and three young children were right behind the ambulance and had been directed to the waiting room. All of this was typical for such situations.

Like the well-oiled machine we were, we went to work as a team.

Your best chance of survival in such scenarios is in the first 1 to 10 minutes. With someone so young and otherwise healthy, the odds of viable survival start to improve even with a longer downtime; however, very slightly. So, with younger adults and children, most healthcare teams will go well beyond what the book says. But with already 40 minutes down time before arrival, even this was beyond the norm. Normally, we would go 2 to 3 rounds of the usual medications while continuing CPR to circulate, continue to maintain their airway, get some of the stat lab results, maybe try some not usual medications, and if there is no response after another 15 to 20 minutes, call it a day and notify the family.

Next case.

As with almost every physician running such a scenario, which we call simply a "code", after 20 minutes or so, the physician asked if there were any objections for any team members to "calling the code".

Now, I have been through countless codes, people of all ages, shapes and sizes. I never once raised my hand, so to speak, and said no, let's keep going. Remember, now we have a downtime of at least an hour of no response to all best efforts; this is way beyond the statistical norm. Even if now we get a response, the best CPR is not the same circulation as a normal beating heart, air exchange is really minimal, and even at this point, if we do get a response, the likelihood of this young mother having any meaningful brain function is almost nil. But some voice told me, no, don't give up. So I spoke up. I simply said, 2 more rounds. As I said it, this didn't make sense even to me, but out it came. So we continued.

Another round of drugs continued CPR in rotation. After a while, CPR gets tiring, I don't care how in shape you are. And as we go to give the second round, sure enough, we get a pulse. A physical response, finally. We adjust the drips, get another EKG, and, within a minute or two, start registering blood pressure. This was amazing. Almost unheard of. But it was true.

Once we managed to get her more stabilized, the Doctor went out to speak to the family, the team helped clean up the room, I was constantly adjusting the drips, and I now had my one and only patient to focus on until an ICU bed became available. A few hours later, a bed became available, and we transferred our miracle patient to the ICU, wondering if she would ever wake up and, if she did, what her mental capabilities would be.

Next, patient, move on.

I didn't think much more of it at the time, though I was proud to be a part of this miracle, until, about 10 days later, I saw her husband come into the ER. He approached me and simply shook my hand to thank me. Behind him, in the hall in a wheelchair, was his wife, our patient. Not only was she able to go home, but she also showed no mental deficits.

To this day, I can't think of, speak of, or write about this case without becoming deeply emotional. This woman is likely alive today, raising her children, celebrating their special moments, and living a normal life because of the incredible team we had that day—and because I trusted and followed that inner voice. The weight of that memory and the impact of our actions still move me profoundly.

About the Author

Keith Matthews, RN, is a dedicated Hospice nurse based in northern Florida. Originally a mathematics major, Keith's career took a transformative turn when he began working in a hospital Emergency Room. His diverse experience spans various settings, including multiple emergency rooms, critical care units, a recovery room, a cardiac cath lab, and a Level One trauma center in New Jersey. After relocating from New Jersey over 25 years ago, Keith has built his life in Florida, where he raised his family. His sons are Alberto, a musician and business owner in St. Augustine, and Richard, who serves in the U.S. Air Force. His daughter, Madison, a Florida State University alumna, is currently pursuing her nursing degree at the University of North Florida. Keith now resides in St. Augustine with his new wife, Dr. Julie Graves.

www.ingramcontent.com/pod-product-compliance
Ingram Content Group UK Ltd.
Pitfield, Milton Keynes, MK11 3LW, UK
UKHW062256290726
14090UKWH00017B/719